THE UNMAKING OF THE BLACK MAN

BY

GIBRAN TARIQ

ACKNOWLEDGEMENTS

So very proud to announce that my oldest daughter became a doctor today (6/14/18). At precisely 2:00 pm, she officially completed the requirements for her doctorate and is now Dr. LaTonya M. Summers. CONGRATS!!!

I also would like to acknowledge three people who had a tremendous impact on my life. My cousin, Marian, who would take me to the movies when I was very young, and then ask me to write about it. She taught me how to play Scrabble, and gave me her collection of Mad magazines. Secondly, Mr. Maurice Baker, my 8th grade history teacher at Polk Youth Center in Raleigh, NC. He thrilled me with his knowledge of words. He was like a walking dictionary, and he influenced me a lot. And Mrs. Joan Boudreax who believed in me. I have never met anyone like her in my life, and I'm grateful for all she taught me in her prison journalism class.

Chapter One

THE BIG PICTURE

Whatever your religious beliefs, it will pretty much be agreed upon that God's first gift to man was image. It appears in most religious literature that just as soon as the Creator, in His infinite wisdom, decided to divide the earthly realms into beasts and humans, He immediately set man upon his first evolutionary turning point. He created man in His own image. Therefore, before man was officially endowed with any other faculty, he had an image and perhaps, above all, a divine image that would be unimpeachable since it did indeed derive from God Himself.

Image, then was undoubtedly the first serious connection between God and man, and it was thus possible to believe that no earthly changes would ever alter the definition of who man was although man could reduce the character of his image by allowing himself to become the object of his image rather than its subject.

At any rate, in antiquity, during religion's most confident age, at least up to the time before physical differences became the yardstick that separated people, what first divided men was how well they wore their image, namely if you were a believer or a heretic. Thusly, it was your god-image—the ability to tie yourself to what God had ordained—that was the first written

1

justification that promoted the legitimacy of one group of men governing another.

However, in the last days of man's early spiritual enfranchisement, and again just before the empire-building of the Greeks, the question of image underwent some "humanitarian" changes to satisfy man's need for conquest and plunder, both of which appeared very ungodlike. And since no king, or member of the church was bold enough to justify rape and pillage as being in the interests of God, they set forth the pretext that it was acceptable to conceive of image as a bodily condition instead of a spiritual one.

Now, that man was free to reinvent himself, all of a sudden, questions of differences had a physical basis. What naturally followed was the establishment of a human "cult of personality" where men consciously took on the attributes of their kings and rulers. As can be imagined, and it was inevitable, that once men sought to alter their image from Godlike to man-made, superiority would be determined by the sword.

Spiritual image collapsed at the end of the sword as did the innumerable traditions about brotherly love since the heirs of this innovative thought found survival was much easier when pursuing an offensive policy than a defensive one. What happened then was that image was established as the prelude to "Might make right" These were history's first made-men.

BONFIRE BOOKS

The state of image was, however, somewhat different in the animal kingdom----but no less important. In fact, the goodness and the glory of the animal world hinged as much on image as anything else. It was also equally true that the power of a strong image was coveted because from the point of view of a hungry predator, it could signify either life or death

In the animal world, it was image that determined something as natural as who got sex or something as important as who got food so similarly the beasts of the field discovered that a certain image prevented them from abuse, or provided them with privilege. And this info was passed on from offspring to offspring for the sole purpose of self-preservation.

Acting in imitation of their elders, young creatures employed the same behavioral traits, learning to bare their fangs, to beat their chests, or to flash their colors to establish the suitable image that would insure their longevity.

In the human world, there is not the least bit of mysticism surrounding longevity, and in most cultures longevity and immortality are practically synonymous with the fashion of passing down image, the most essential element in the communication of culture expressed among peoples. Wherever the culture of image is lost among a people, they perish.

Amongst blacks, the tradition evaporated, and quite naturally, this was a terrible thing because just like that, we became unmade men.

Chapter Two

COWBOYS AND COLORED FOLKS

Black folks must know the truth. Since the dawn of slavery, image has been one of the most vital building blocks of racism in this country. In every segment of this society, image has been the naturally occurring poison that has both promoted and upheld segregation, the scourge that has power-driven the American people to the present societal crossroads.

What makes image so deceptive is its ability to perpetuate the illusion that one-size-fits-all. Sadly, this country has literally become the symbolic playing field for the expression of using one negative image as a promotional tool to cast suspicions upon others similarly situated.

Although a leader in the field, this nation is not the only one to employ image as a social engineering tool, and since nothing else is as easy to manipulate as image, one can isolate an entire group simply by the process of what I term 'interactive networking'. The principle is so complete that when you inject a single, negative image, you can, with only minor tinkering, command that image to consume a host of other unrelated people.

Wanna see how it works? Okay, it doesn't take much to figure out what the media is trying to express when it addresses the capture of a criminal by flashing not just images of the suspected individual, but also of his family, friends, and neighborhood. With certainty, the family is implicated. By turn, the friends of the accused are subliminally guilty by association since it is assumed they harbor the same criminal tendencies, and the 'hood is subconsciously indicted as a 'breeding ground' for such illegal behavior. Therefore, a single negative image can go far beyond the original assumption of a crime being committed to a social question about group characteristics. This is so because when the evening news is permitted to incorporate as much unrelated image dynamics onto what is in fact an isolated incident, then subconscious connections are made. For blacks, there are no safety valves when white America's 'shock quotient' intersects with black America's 'threat quotient'.

The same thing that makes the media so powerful in the artificial world of entertainment is the same thing that makes it so powerful in the real world: the power to control---or to distort---images. But there is also another more problematic threat because what is most bedeviling is that image invents the relentless need to 'breed' stories to regulate their effects, and such stories serve to give the image a boost every time it is viewed. Rarely, if ever, are people disciplined enough to view an image and not recount the accompanying tale. How difficult is it to view an image of Jesus and not see his pedigree? What about a brotha in an orange jailhouse jumpsuit? Both images are spiritually strapped to our psyche with storyline intact.

For many of us from earlier generations, without even a slight shift in our perspective, we have reserved a place in our collective memory that pairs the physical beauty of a sista in a hat with church. We don't even have to struggle with the connection because the sheer power of awareness continually defines the map of our consciousness to the point where we no longer encounter the world as is, but as we experience it from memory. What this means is that we stake our humanity on conjecture, on what we have known, and consequently, we never live beyond what's visible.

Added to this insight is the process of habit since any time a people perceives their environment via memory, there is no degree of separation between conscious action and habit. And for our evolutionary purposes, this must be recognized as extraordinarily regressive. Why" Because whenever close families and extended neighborhoods reside in close proximity to any crippling memory, that people will shape their survival around that memory, and then will suit their habits to satisfy that memory.

Case in point. Unarguably, black folks continually shape their passive behavior towards white folks because we remember slavery, lynch mobs, Jim Crow, and the KKK. Via memory, we have gained the habit of being submissive, and since evolution is a slow process, we still haven't discovered how to defuse our memories, or how to de-energize our fears.

For brothas and sistas, this is most unfortunate since all social interactions are cued from memory. What else is important to remember is that since memory sketches the visceral pictures that has kept us in our place, it also compels us to live habit-shaped lives. Fundamentally, habits are neither hard-working nor heroic, yet they instruct us on how we should view ourselves, and how we should relate to the world at large.

The purpose of a habit is to be as precise as clockwork, and since we have no historical memory of ever being treated fairly by white America, our collective habits urge us to use the same universal method that all vulnerable species have forever employed when in contact with a superior species------passive submissiveness. In essence, we 'bitch up'. And that has been our image.

Moreover, the image of a brotha standing meekly before the white man with hat in hand is perhaps the most fear-inspired image ever recorded, and not only does white America enjoy the rewards of this negative image, but it has also served as the burial rites for our collective manhood.

Image rules!

BONEFIRE BOOKS

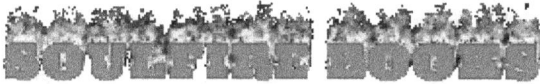

We now recognize that white America, if it was to enslave an entire race for all of eternity, had to develop image-producing skills unmatched in the universe. How else would their power be revealed, or our hopelessness invented.

It is possible that the science of image-assassination began some time before the Willie Lynch era, but the study was considerably expanded during this time when it became anchored to scientific methodology. It wasn't that Europeans, prior to Willie Lynch, had guessed wrong about screwing together a program to manufacture slaves out of men, but if slavery was going to last, forward-thinking white men understood the techniques must be refined.

In earlier times, slave-masters possibly thought of slavery as a condition of circumstances that could be measured by war, remedied by ransom, and understood by all, but entering the 17th century, the science of slavery gathered momentum, but did not become painstakingly exact until "image" qualified the process. Prior to this model, slave-breakers had experienced with a variety of "taming" techniques: beatings, and torture among them, along with the fathomless craft of stripping away one's culture. Yet, against these gloomy odds, some of the Africans miraculously resisted transformation. No matter how vicious or cruel the technique, these Africans, though dehumanized, could resurrect themselves.

An African warrior, as long as he maintained the "image" of himself as a warrior, would resist and fight. Even stripped of his culture, deprived of his religion, and placed on foreign soil, it would still not matter because even without these things, the warrior would still remain a warrior. He could still focus because he still possessed an image of himself.

By inventing an image of the African that was beyond the range of his experience, the slave-makers forced the Africans to accept unqualified and unsubstantiated assumptions about themselves, and thus it began. Almost.

Pulled by the enormity of a task this complex, the slave-masters set out on a revolutionary quest to unravel the mysterious phenomena of image, but there was one thing more he needed to do to fulfil his quest. He had to hatch an image of himself that was bigger than life, and for this he decided to invent for himself the most spectacular image on earth; he painted Jesus white!

Actually, the image of Jesus had already been painted some time before this, but the image had lost none of its impact when Euro-Americans needed a visage on which to hang their godliness. This bleached image of Jesus was, for the white man, a godsend. And like all sensationalism with a lie at its core, the myth proved adequate to the task at hand.

It is very conceivable that our future would have been a lot more promising had the Jesus myth been exposed and openly challenged since so much of the white man's dream was attached to it. If black preachers would have looked a little deeper into our history, he could have easily poked holes into this fuzzy logic.

Practically every Christmas, preachers everywhere celebrate the Nativity, and swoop and swoon over how the baby Jesus was on King Herod's hit list, and how God saved him. It's right here that black ministers, with all their education, should have known that The Creator, in His Infinite Wisdom, should have known precisely what He was doing. If God sent Jesus into black Egypt for the sole purpose of saving him, then that would mean that Jesus would have had to have looked like the people of Egypt. After all, it would be extremely difficult to hide a giraffe among a flock of sheep. An equally compelling case can be made against the likelihood of successfully hiding a human being among other humans with whom he shared none of the same racial traits.

Did God somehow misplace Jesus. Not hardly. God knew exactly what the people of Egypt looked like, so in order to justify the decision to send Jesus into Egypt, this meant, specifically, that this baby had to, by necessity, look like the Egyptians!

At present, the Jesus Factor is the most profound socio/political link in our evolutionary regression, and in the centuries following this myth, white America, using the trickle down strategy imposed other pseudo-super Caucasian characters upon our consciousness. Tarzan, Santa Claus, and Uncle Sam are nothing more than caricatures of Jesus, the first white superhero.

Has this image caused problems? Sure it has, but it is even more profound. Ever since the advent of sliced bread, we have had to contend with white arrogance and supremacy. In the same manner that they white-washed Jesus, they "purified" bread, sugar, rice, grits, etc. by whitening them, and then commercialized these 'zero nutrition' foods as superior. In recent years, scientists have demonstrated the worthlessness of these bleached products.

But imagine having the power, as the white man did, to have the pleasure of looking at everything and seeing yourself. But wasn't that the point? To have the power to transform your beauty into art, into science, and then to transpose it upon everything.

Chapter Three

UNDER PRESSURE

Freedom, no doubt, transformed overnight, the status of the black man into an unknown, dark void where he would be compelled-----nay coerced---- to evolve out of his one-dimensional slave persona into a fully developed human being.

Although the pattern of a people starting over again had been repeated countless times throughout history, this was the first time it would be attempted by a people born blind because without the "hereditary gift" of image, the newly-freed slaves would have to invent a new way of life to survive against great odds.

Without image, the ex-slaves had to rely on memory to chronicle their new history, but when it came to remembering, what was there except convulsive reminders of their abject powerlessness? Surely, our chances at renewal would have been better had we possessed a positive image of ourselves to draw upon.

During France's dark years, when the country was occupied for four years by German troops, what held the country together despite their defeat in war was the image of themselves as a great society. They took great pride in the French national identity, and they rallied behind their flag, and other cultural symbols that were deeply rooted in their collective psyche.

Even Germany, after its defeat in WWI, made a perch for itself upon their national image, and was able, in a very short time, to roll up their perceived dishonor at Versailles, and to rejuvenate itself.

The Jewish people, after suffering the Holocaust, were enabled by their image of "the chosen ones" to overcome, and to rebuild.

In contrast, African-Americans had no image, no national identity to fall back on, and without an image to spell out our mission, we had nothing to aspire to. We had no glory to recapture, or no honor to reclaim. Instead, we were without vision. Thus, with blacks, a new standardized response to suffering was introduced which marked both a defining moment as well as a turning point in our evolution.

After enduring the atrocities of slavery, in what was to be the first full-scale attempt at black genocide, we opted for individualism. Invariably, though, not surprising, blacks pretty much celebrated their release from bondage by going their own ways, something so unconventional and contrary that it defied reason.

The whole point of freedom.......Well, there should have never been a puzzle to freedom, and the very steps should have been to remain intact as a collective, and then to evolve into a community. In practice, individualism was the greatest blow to the stability of the blossoming black community.

Partly through progressive individualism, we failed to establish a coherent set of values that would have been conducive to the development of a positive image. Additionally, following the Great Migration, black America evolved into a pluralistic society with each half only willing to invest in their own self-interests.

In the south, thanks to Jim Crow, place was not a spooky question, or one requiring any guesswork, and as an added incentive, lynching helped provide the black man with the "know-how" to stay in his place.

Southern life for the brotha was guided solely by the church. The southern black man looked to Jesus to give him land to plow, to keep the white man in check, and when this failed, to make sure he got his crown in the ol'-bye-and-bye.

But something else was happening with the black man. No sooner had the first stage of the black demographic resettlement taken place than the dark transplants encountered living of a sort they had never experienced before en masse. At no time in the history of the black man had he ever been compelled to adjust to an urban environment, and in many senses, this was revolutionary.

The urban change was, at once, disheartening. Black people forever had a tradition of living close to the soil, and this congestion of ghetto was a truly novel experience, so much so that in conjunction to finding an image, blacks in the north also had to find an identity.

In the north, the idea of consumerism spread like a new gospel, and hedged in by their very first contact with the possession of the almighty dollar, blacks practiced spending with a spiritual zeal. They, at least, had found an identity: CONSUMERS!

SOULFIRE BOOKS

Nothing worse erupted out of the mythical Emancipation Proclamation than the vulgar manner by which black people were routinely brutalized, tortured, and murdered. No less awful was the little known Pig Law of 1876. Imagine this. The view of a free-to-roam black man was too vast for a white America that was eager to restrain him, so it seemed only sensible to vilify him----and then to imprison him.

The infamous Pig Law, in all honesty, is the equivalent of today's crack law. It had the same social impact. Once the white man lost the right to hold the black man hostage on the plantation, he knew that, by principle, he had to rely on another device to hold him down. What happened was that immediately after the slaves were set free, the law made the stealing of a pig or any sort of farm animal valued at ten dollars an offense punishable as grand larceny which carried a five year prison term. Just the week before, stealing a pig would have, at best, gotten a brotha a whipping by the slave-master, but after Emancipation----it was lockdown. With no place to go, and no food to eat, the newly-freed slave arrest rate began, and in the years between 1870 and 1910, the black prison population grew 10 times faster than the general population.

Was there any justification for this transition from the plantation to prison? To white America, necessity had them bending over backwards in an effort to maintain control of the black man, so once laws were shaped to suit their purposes, white America replaced the mumbo-jumbo of what a free nigga wasn't with a custom-made image of what he was. The results were not pretty.

Still, their early attempts to portray the black man as the biggest threat to national security would makes us chuckle today, but it was good that the white man had a sense of humor. How else would they have promoted the image of the black man as being lazy!

What audacity! The black man had just finished building the entire south, and the white man labels him as good for nothing. That image of the black man should never found support from anyone, yet this was white America's very first negative image of the post-slavery black man.

Add to this cultural nicety, the fact that the black man would steal the stink out of shit, and that he had a thing for white women, and overnight, he became Public Enemy #1.

Chapter Four

SHITTING WHERE YOU SLEEP

In the 18h century, white America had a simple view of the world which allowed it to do two things at once. The first was to expand its influence abroad. The second was to keep the black man in his place. One need not spend any time puzzling over the success of either as history bears witness to his triumphs.

Once white America began to hawk our image in a negative fashion, and prison became a ceremonial plantation, black men reacted in much the same way as we had reacted to slavery, and we do so in the same odd manner-----by showing we could take it.

This had, by now, become a tradition with black males. No matter what the white man dished out, we would simply grit our teeth and tough it out just to prove we could take whatever he threw at us. Somehow, we wrongly surmised that as long as we survived that we had won. This was notably so during slavery. We survived so must have won.

This tradition of Pyrrhic victory is still alive and well today, most noticeably among brothas in the joint. No matter how much time the system gives, or how harsh the conditions of their confinement, they declare themselves the victor if they survive it. Rather than fighting the system that gave them the time, or rather than attacking the brutal conditions of prison, they instead focus on being strong, to prove to the system that they can take it.

And while it may be absurd to view this souped-up masculinity as a black cultural happening, it would be as equally foolish to ignore the degree to which this notion has helped to define the current trend of violence that is so intimately bound up in the identity of today's black youth. Yet, almost as soon as the Hip-Hop generation inherited and accepted the super-macho grin-and-bear-it mystique, they knew they had made a mistake. In practice, they loved being tough, but their idea of toughness had little in common with the heroic stoicism of their elders. These young ones would bridge the cultural chasm with gunsmoke. Sadly, however, the gun would be turned on themselves.

At this point, we must remind ourselves that today's 'black gunsmoke' culture did not grow out of the challenges of the Black Power Movement although there is the social perspective that our fascination with guns occurred during this period.

Though the Black Power Movement was less privileged than the Civil Rights Movement, a popular culture grew up around both as it has the Hip-Hop Movement, and critical to the understanding of these movements, especially the first two, it must be recalled that one was largely based on the concept of progress while the other made a dramatic departure by demanding change, and in so doing, The Black Power Movement defined a new relationship with white America. And it was one that inspired fear in them, something they hadn't experienced that viscerally since Brother Nat Turner.

From out of the activities of the 60s, aspects of a black image developed. The scowling, unsmiling image of the black man had its origins in The Nation of Islam although these Muslims kept their affairs private, and never hardly expressed their political views publicly. No matter, The Nation of Islam, with its stern outward demeanor, presented the first peek at an image evolved from a black perspective that was not characterized by submissiveness.

The Black Power Movement then utilized the stern image of The Nation of Islam, but undertook "kicking ass" as a development of their own, and the conscious decision to fight back allowed them greater control of this new, black image. Via The Black Panther Party, this new militant image, coupled with the afro and the raised, clenched fist suddenly became the urban logo.

As can be imagined, the US government eagerly resorted to low-intensity warfare as a social mechanism of ethnic cleansing. Yet despite COINTELPRO, and the killing and imprisonments that followed in its wake, when the US saw they were powerless to destroy this powerful, black image by either gunfire or legal oppression, they decided to fight fire with fire. And it was this shift in tactics that gave them the victory they so badly sought.

Just at what point the government realized it couldn't continue this endemic war against its so-called citizens is unclear, but what was clear is that in 1972, Uncle Sam decided that instead of attacking the institution of the image, they would attack the distortion.

After centuries of a servile black man, white folks felt that the militant image of the black man was a gross distortion, and all they had to do to set things right would be to simply correct this distorted image. Therefore, they turned to Hollywood-----the premier image-maker.

Would Hollywood be up the task? The movie industry had always functioned under a primitive sort of democracy that had relegated blacks to menial, servile roles, and it was this old-time Hollywood image that helped foster the image of happy-go-lucky buffoons. So it was only natural that the control of the black image would once again revert to Hollywood, and what resulted was SuperFly, The Mack, and the whole Blaxploitation genre.

The impact was both startling and immediate. Viewing themselves on the big screen for the first time was a thousand times more revolutionary than the revolution itself. The revolution had just been hijacked. Suddenly, the images of Rap Brown, and Huey Newton morphed into the more colorful images of Priest(SuperFly] and Goldie{The Mack]. Accordingly, the hood was no longer a battlefield. Instead it was a commercialized stomping grounds where everyone became both prey and predator. Black on Black crime had just grown another head.

Prior to this, black crime had always been structured around the premise that "the white man was always the victim". In the hood, the old heads would hip the young crooks not to ever take from another black. The deal was to do Mr. Charlie. However, these movies ushered in the notion that "all money was good money", and for the first time, blacks victimized each other on a grand scale, and once we began to shit where we slept, we became invested with an image that took the white folks off the hook------and put us on it.

SOULFIRE BOOKS

The theory goes that the road to our self-hatred had been paved long before this, and that the black on black crime that was an offshoot of this mentality had actually been seeded with the actions of a tiny elite: the integrationists, and the athletes.

With hindsight, we all realize that integration was not the sacred cow black leaders had hoped it would be. For some reason, integrationists, acted on the principle that our problems would be solved by living next door to Mr. Charlie and Miss Ann. Never had our leaders been so wrong.

1964.

In 1964, American politics were a constitutional hodge-podge, and it is highly unlikely that Congress was unaware of what would ultimately happen once HUD {Housing and Urban Development}, without ceremony, crashed the gates of black America to raze the slums to the ground.

More than anything else, the cranes and the bulldozers should have been welcomed, and the demolition crews applauded as hard-hat heroes. They weren't.

What happened next was social genocide, the heady stench of white folks trying to perform a miracle of doing good to a people they didn't know a damn thing about. Sometimes, the charity of white people can be a harrowing experience.

When the urban renewal program came thundering through the hood in 1964, the bulldozers, which were the precious toys of integration, also knocked over black, family life because white researchers failed to recognize how tight-knit black communities were at that time.

Despite all the lavish spending to integrate blacks into the social fabric of America was socially spoiled because no one wanted the black youth------except white coaches! For them, integration was a sports bonanza, and at last they had gotten access to the fabled nigga athlete. Dreams of a sports dynasty danced in their heads.

To the black urban male, sports was the most masculine endeavor he could envision, but white coaches re-created the values these youth had been taught to cherish. Everywhere in the hood from the preachers, the pimps, playas, and coaches, the youngbloods were taught the etiquette of black sportsmanship. *You never kicked a man when he was down; you never hit below the belt; you always gave a man a fair fight.*

In the hustling world, it was preached that you never took a man's last, and that you always gave him a little something to go home with. This was "street" wisdom and there was nothing shabby about it. Even as a foe, the black man was first and foremost, a brotha.

The atmosphere in the white world was totally different, a complete reversal of the teachings in the black community. White coaches preached the theory that coming in second was for suckers, that you win at all costs, that it was your duty as an athlete to succeed by any means necessary. You kicked your opponent when you had him down, you punched him in the balls, and you took everything he had.

The quality and diversity of this new gospel sounded exotic to the black youth who swallowed it up, figuring that, at long last, they had found the Holy Grail, the esoteric knowledge that had granted the white man the power to do all the great things they had done. The black athlete felt privileged to finally have this key to success because if these pearls of wisdom had worked so well for the white man, surely they would work for him. And it was then that black neighborhoods became the testing grounds for these new-fangled teachings.

Like the Golden Horde that poured out of the Mongolian steppes, black athletes, already aggressive, bum-rushed the hood and turned it inside out. Learning from scratch, these brothas went about the destruction of black America with uncommon arrogance. Methodically, these brothas sought out the rules to becoming king-of-the-hill with the same intensity of an Einstein in search of the theory of relativity, or a Newton hunting for the laws of gravity.

For the first time, blacks made it a career to taking advantage of other blacks. Even during slavery, the question of stealing from another black was a not a question at all. It was a foregone conclusion. We did not take from one another! Taking from the white man could never-----under any circumstances-----be deemed stealing. It was stealing only when you took from another black.

Before 1964, and the teachings, most black on black crime were crimes of passion; unfortunate lover's quarrels, or juke joint murder where the liquor got to talking a little too loudly. Hardly ever did blacks prey on one another, if not out of brotherly love, then out of the notion that "niggas ain't have shit worth taking noway."

Either way, black property was safe from the hands of other blacks.

True enough, we started shitting where we laid our heads.

Chapter Five

THE OTHER END OF THE STICK

The social revolution for the control of the black image had a profound impact on the sistas as well. Oppression was not solely a franchise for the black male because harnessed to his very existence was the black woman. After 1865, once she was no longer needed as a breeder of slaves, she posed a definite threat. After all, she was the producer of the one thing the white man hated most in the world---the black man.

By the start of the 19th century, the black woman was no longer viewed as a "transitional" figure in the dark menace. She was the producer of it. And as the creator of this scourge, what to do about her only became a matter of timing.

All things considered, white America exercised uncommon restraint regarding the black woman. That, considering their disdain for her sons, was admirable. Initially, white tolerance was exemplified by the government's ban on having more than two children, and while this was a blanket decree to all women, it was no doubt a nasty strike at the black population explosion. Yet, black births continued.

Once it became apparently clear that black procreation couldn't be legislated, a vicious sterilization program was enacted.

By the mid 1930s, under the banner of Psychiatry's Racial Purity Law, over 15,000 sterilizations were performed in this country, mainly by Dr. Lorthup Stoppard, an avowed racist, who believed what he was doing was humanitarian.

In 1939, the founder of Planned Parenthood, Margaret Sanger, proposed a plan to eliminate black babies. She hired black preachers with "engaging personalities" to spread the message that sterilization was the solution for poverty. However, just before this phase of the sterilization project could kick off, worldwide protests shut it down as a human rights violation. America would be forced to halt its sterilization program------or to justify it.

Conveniently, it was around this time that the concept of IQ was used by Uncle Sam to continue his project under the guise of "scientific justification". Within a short time, Lewis Terman, declared that blacks were so feeble-minded that they should not be allowed to reproduce. Now, with so-called scientific justification, the program finally had legs, and in New Orleans, black prisoners were experimented on, and given electrode implants. The psycho-surgery performed by Dr. Robert Heath of Tulane University bragged that "niggers were cheaper to use in experiments than cats because niggers were everywhere."

Not wanting to miss all the fun, the CIA funded the infamous Dr. Heath to conduct LSD experiments on brothas in the Louisiana State Penitentiary. Not to be outdone, The National Institute of Mental Health got their licks in by feeding brothas a drug, B3, which was 100 times more powerful than LSD. Some of the brothas hallucinated for 77 days in a row!

The Civil Rights Movement helped little as <u>The Mental Retardation Facilities and Communities Health Centers Ac</u>t was passed in 1963 which placed black school children at great peril. Funded by NIMH, and founded by Dr. Robert Felix, this was white America's boldest strike against brothas and sistas. This time, they were going for our jugular-----the children. The government, at every level, gave Felix the absolute power to administer powerful psychotropic drugs known to induce aggressive and violent behavior

Dr. Felix's Mental Health Center's Act put psychologists and psychiatrists in public schools in ever-growing numbers, and as the numbers increased, the SAT scores decreased. All at once, teachings about morals, ethics, and human cooperation were substituted with a new "value clarification" system devised by who else---the psychiatrists. These programs led to a moral decline as students were conditioned to choose personal choice over social responsibility.

And this was merely Headstart. In 1965, "Special Education" classes were established via the US Elementary and Secondary Education Act. Now, let's pause for a bit of reflection. In 1930, 80% of African-Americans over 14 could read. Sixty years later, after twenty-five years of Special Ed, only 56% of the black population could read. Since Dr. Felix, the suicide rate for brothas, 15-19, has zoomed. Surprised. Well, it was known that the drugs would result in violent and suicidal behavior

On any other planet, it would be astounding that a nation that had tricked unsuspecting black kids into taking mind-altering drugs known to cause violence would a decade or so later want to hunt them down because they were violent and irrational.

Additionally, when Lonnie J. West, a psychiatrist, formerly of UCLA's Neuropsychiatric Institute, preached that the violence of black, urban males was genetic, he also recommended castration as a remedy. It was only after nationwide protests that federal funding dried up, but it was revived in 1982 when Duke University's

Medical School was provided funding to study aggression in black children.

A report by the African-American Coalition for Justice in Social Policy indicates that NIMH's research parallels the skyrocketing violence in the hood. Jim Brewer of the Coalition stated that "most of the violence in the last three decades has been the results of experiments in the form of drug therapy and psychological school programs. These have ravaged our inner cities and manufactured criminals out of young people, all because we unwittingly allowed psychiatrists and psychologists to study behavior in our schools instead of leaving teachers to teach education." If you, by now, entertain the notion that we have been set up, then welcome to the club.

COVERTURE BOOKS

And what about the beloved black woman? No doubt, she still represented a sizable threat, and there was no great willingness on the part of white America to insanely believe the 'black male' problem could be effectively neutralized or fixed by their pet projects (sterilization, mental health centers, prisons) so they had, by necessity, to adopt a more proactive approach when it came to dealing with the black woman's complicity.

Here is the essential point. And in all fairness, it must be understood that the black woman, like the black man, is a finished product of white racism, so at best, many of her reactions/responses are instinctual/automatic. Having said that, the black woman is 'possessed' with the most idealized concept of the white man as a savior-in-waiting. To the older sista, it's Jesus. To the sista in the 'hood, it's Uncle Sam with his welfare checks. And to the young sista, it's Santa Claus. Sadly, this super-sized Mighty Whitey image is still alive and well in certain circles.

What's worse is that sistas are extremely disillusioned with brothas-----or at least our capacity to address, or even better yet, to satisfy their expectations of us. Since day one, there has been little doubt about what black women wanted. Sistas have always demanded security, and had every reason to initially believe that we would be able to sponsor the notion. And why not? The black woman was no idle spectator in what black men had done for the white man. She, indeed, was a personal witness to the manner in which we had labored to grow this country from nothing. She, with her own eyes, had seen the magic emanate from our hands as we had conjured up crops from a barren earth. At no point was the sista absent as we went about the business of making cities out of wilderness, of making cotton king, or of making the white man wealthy. So after this visual testimony, how could the black woman expect less from us.

Chapter Six

*The Blank Slate/Full Plate
Syndrome*

One of the primary difficulties facing the post-slavery black female was the ability to make herself feminine. Slavery, no doubt, where sistas had toiled in the fields as long and as hard as the brothas, rewarded her nothing due to gender. Sure, sistas gave birth and, for a period, raised children, but more times than not, the major characteristic of sex was to breed which was simply another chore to be performed.

The en of slavery should have brought about, for sistas, a return to femininity, but just what was it? After a lengthy 250 years of being treated as chattel property with no true opportunity to grow psychologically as a woman, black women had no clear knowledge of the African rituals and customs that defined womanhood, and since black womanhood was heretofore unknown on these shores, sistas were left with a blank slate on which to define themselves. But how was this to be accomplished? Since she had worked as an equal in the back-breaking work of the field, had shared equally the horror of servitude, had eaten the same coarse food, and had worn equally coarse, unflattering clothes, did sistas demand full equality with brothas. Or did they borrow heavily from Miss Ann, the slave mistress which provided the only comprehensive view of womanhood that black women had ever seen. Either way, ultimately, black women would be compelled to become feminine, and essentially this shift in perspective would be as traumatic for sistas as learning to be breadwinners would be for the brothas. For certain, both these factors had an obvious impact on the complexities of black life today.

Notwithstanding anything else, black women had to acknowledge that the essence of womanhood did not evolve from the authority of their vaginas because on the other side of their fertility, there were such subtle cues as hair, makeup, nails, and attire whose proper use tended to legitimize the arts of femininity.

Since sistas had no experience in this, the fine arts of femininity would have to arise out of the black woman's imitation of Miss Ann since they possessed nothing from their personal experiences as slaves that would or could provide them the wealth of information required to become more than ritualistic caricatures of true womanhood. Titties and ass only set men off in pursuit of them sexually, and though physical assets may not have offered the true secrets of femininity, they became the initial building blocks of black femininity. With not much else, titties and ass became the physical electives that awarded sistas the 'everlasting life' of womanhood.

The invention of a black femininity, never accomplished before in the new world would not be easy following a lifestyle of being a sexual object. Additionally, when compared to Miss Ann, sistas could not identify anything about themselves that would brand them as sexy. Their entire image was organized around the 'plantation mammy', an apron-wearing, dirty-faced, rag-headed matron. Surely, no pin-up model, and hardly the ideal on which to base their collective feminine worth. And what of the ethical behavior that would, most definitely, have to accompany the new, black femininity? Sistas simply could not establish an image withut the underlying ethics to maintain it since the freedom to be true to themselves would be more a condition of good decision-making rather than physical attributes.

What would be crucial when black women made their new covenant with themselves would be---for the most part---how much slavery had affected their opinion of themselves on three very vital levels. They undoubtedly would have to determine how bondage had affected them as (1) humans,(2) as women, and (3) as black. And since all three were so closely related to their most innate sense of being, anything that had happened during slavery, which could not be rationalized or repressed on any level, would inhibit them from being complete or healed.

There can be no argument that bondage was an unique experience for the black woman, one where her capacity as a human was ignored, her womanhood denounced, and her blackness pronounced a curse. Admittedly, not much to kindle optimism, but the sista had to be reborn out of these ashes, but what kind of self-worth could possibly evolve from a prior life where she had been a possession of the white man, and an obsession to the black man?

SOULFIRE BOOKS

While other little girls all over the world dreamed of Prince Charming, the young slave sista dreamed of a savior. And given the position of the brotha, it was almost certain that her vision of a deliverer was not black. It was this messianic complex that hemmed the sista into the Jesus Superstar Syndrome where it was much easier for her to ultimately view the white man as a source of admiration which helps to explain the importance of the white man, Mr. Charlie, in the authentic history of sistahood. Moreover, what was indicative of this image of the white man as first among equals was the incalculable risk of her drawing a conclusion on her blank slate that emasculated the brothas.

A point to ponder: A blank slate will bring about a full plate which means, simply put, that if you cannot devise your own rules, you will be compelled to play by the rules of someone else.

Now, several significant factors emerged during the early post-slavery days that resulted in the downfall of the black household. In general, the vulnerability of the black household was further aggravated by the white man who was the primary instrument of the discord. This was a high-water mark because it revealed that it was possible for the white man to control what went on inside the black household by using the black woman as an unknowing agent of his 'scorched earth' policy against the brrotha. Two areas were of immediate concern. (1) The financial capacity of the black man, and (2) the black woman's overall image of him. By controlling the job market, it was a relatively simple task for white America to limit the earnings of black men. Well, there was no problem with the white image.

In the early 1900s, the black woman was still playing connect-a-dot on her blank slate so it became easy to unwittingly recruit her to curb the enthusiasm and ambition of the black man. Increasingly, by the mid-1900s, white America had come to view the black household as a strategic territory that needed to be destabilized, so by the advent of television, the white man had engineered the most celebrated entry into black America ever devised, and no matter how secure the four walls of his home, the brotha was now powerless to protect himself from Madison Avenue, (the advertising artery of commercial TV) a foe more vicious than Jim Crow.

At the heights of its power, TV broadcast the enormous gap between rich and poor, and as these sistas gawked in open-mouthed awe at the leisure and luxury of the whites on TV, they again criticized the black man for their depressing lifestyle. Meanwhile, the process of diminishing the black man in his own home became more firmly fixed.

In any event, around this time another public policy was institutionalized by white America to strengthen its position in the black household, and in the process to demean the black man. The practice of white bill collectors or door to door salesman identifying the woman as the head of the household was a direct insult to the black male. Invariably, when white strangers demanded to speak with the lady of the house rather than the man, it helped to build a foundation for the black woman to exert authority over the household. When this tactic was attempted in Hispanic communities, the males protested this disrespect in such a fashion that police departments as well as other agencies have been required to take sensitivity or cultural diversity classes in order to understand the inherent disrespect involved in going to a Hispanic residence and requesting an audience with the wife. Black men did nothing in those days to remedy the slight, and like a magic formula, the considerable influence the white men gave them over the household was duly recorded upon the sista's blank slate.

What else happened during this time was that it seemed as if the white man had ordered the mental crucifixion of the black woman via TV. Although tradition holds that the values of the dominant culture will strongly influence the subculture, nothing could account for the subsequent reach and impact of TV which, at once, became the chief advocate of white America's 'good news'.

It was TV that transformed the Euro-American concept of beauty into a gospel, but it also provided the foundation for the destruction of the black woman's self-esteem. Television, which possessed far more power than radio, preserved the beliefs and, in some places, formed the core of an ultra-white system that would become the basis of the 'sex sells' cult.

Unlike radio, which left black women considerable independence, TV made it virtually impossible for sistas to reconcile themselves with any notion/concept of black beauty as many of these early commercials were among the finest promos for the sacrament of white femininity.

As more time passed, the seeming universalism of white values paved the way for the misconception of black beauty. Dark faces on TV seemed a threat to the public order, and only white women were wholesome or beautiful enough to hawk consumer goods on commercials, so virtually overnight, blonde-haired, blue-eyed women came to represent 'the good life' and the products they advertised as an extension of it.

As the TV networks grew, they responded by becoming more exclusive, further undermining the shaky structure of the black household. Furthermore, as the medium grew, it became more apparent to black women that they would never be American beauties. They were, by Hollywood's tradition, ugly.

Something else that came to be during the sista's blank slate period was that since she was still building herself from scratch, she would have nothing to pass on to her daughters. And since her roots were established in the intellectual and cultural heritage of television, what emerged was the origins of today's "Drama Mama".

For most sistas, the most powerful facet of daytime TV was the soap operas, and in a black world where brothas and sistas were basically concerned with survival, the morality of these shows had a great influence on the way black households shaped up. It was only natural, then, that the exotic and exalted doctrines culled from these soaps were ultimately transmitted from mother to daughter, and just as soon as the black oral tradition became peppered with the manufactured examples from TV families, it was as though we had absorbed a pagan culture.

As a student of these 'soaps', black women employed fantasy as a link between her bleak world of despair and the pretty, doll-house world she saw on the tube, and though she knew it was impossible for her to live like the soap opera divas, she could invest her daughters with hope. What resulted was the 'DON'T BE WIT' NO BROKE-ASSED NIGGA" philosophy.

Before long, sistas had added another component to their blank slate, and began to take a positive view of a man's assets, and what did occur was that money and spending power became the criteria used to assess a man's desirability.

During slavery, the black woman exercised little, if any, choice over whom she ended up with, and on those times when she did, her perception of the man was not measured by what he had. Hell, he was a slave---the ultimate broke-assed nigga. Now, however, sistas favored much more in a man, and as the fabled TV commercials offered a dazzling array of consumer choices, they wanted to help put their daughters in a position where they could enjoy them.

The 'don't-be-with-a-broke-nigga' philosophy of the 60s is not specifically the evil sister of today's 'gold-digga' approach favored by many sistas. The former was a statement. The latter is a lifestyle. Both were attempts by black women to escape the worst conditions of life, or at least to improve them.

The slate was no longer blank, and would never be again. TV would see to that.

Chapter Seven

Home Is Where The Hatred Is

Having disposed of the black man's militant image, white America was now about to give life to a new social experiment. It would buy a future for black America, but more realistically, it would pour money into a variety of self-help programs and heavily invest in programs to get blacks into college. This would not have mattered much except that all of this was meant to benefit white society, and it was a prize worth shooting for. Despite drawbacks, the plan was to build the prototype of a new, black man: the suit-and-tie nigga, a buppie.

The strategy was to produce an assembly line of cookie-cutter, black professionals who, it was hoped, would mirror the sentiments and ideals of the dominant culture. The danger was that some of these brothas, once they had gained valuable experience and skills, would refuse to be co-opted by mainstream America, and would go back to the 'hood to provide for the needs of the people there, so the programs had to be geared up in phases.

At one extreme, white America was financing the education of a new generation of blacks, making it easier for them to enter college in record numbers, and this could be dangerous, but at the other extreme, they were incubating an elite class of nigga yes-men whom they could depend on to support the existing status quo. To the establishment, the hardest part would not be in educating them, but in keeping them in line once the needs of the dominant culture had been satisfied. If, of course, that ever happened.

Nevertheless, the accelerated college admissions of African-American students throughout the 70s outfitted black America with its first concentrated wave of its so-called white-educated, black experts, entrepreneurs, and engineers who should have been the answer to black America's prayers, but these 'Oreos' were not mass-produced to make their way back to the ghetto. And none wanted to go back. This in itself should have suggested how deeply they had been miseducated. More appropriately, this educated elite was designed as a booster group for the black middle class that had started to emerge the decade before. Apparently, white folks had enough sense to realize they would need a buffer between them and the masses of poverty-stricken blacks.

BONEFIRE BOOKS

This massive class restructuring resulted in an ironclad caste system where the middle-class were none too eager to take either the money or their knowledge back home as this educated elite, the so-called Talented

THE UNMAKING OF THE BLACK MAN

Tenth, increasingly opted to subscribe to a white lifestyle where the rosiest estimate of their acceptance and self-worth was a white wife. {In a recent magazine article by Harvard Professor Randall Kennedy, he intimated that due to his position and status, it was naturally assumed that he would have a white wife as this was the case with so many other brothers with clout}. At any rate, the reason is not hard to discern. White women were an over-the-counter upgrade.

A very important reason for the development of the black bourgeoisie resulted from the point Karl Marx made over 150 years ago that all change in history comes through the conflict of elements antagonistic to one another. This being so, white America wanted to advance a group to absorb the antagonism their future policies would generate.

The climax of this 'educating' was riveting. It was as though the Euro-centric learning apparatus had cast a spell over these black supplicants, and that they had fallen into a trance from which they could never awaken. In most instances, the brothas' instinct to imitate the white man was so complete that they learned how to walk, talk, and to act Euro, surrendering entirely all Afro-centricisms while doing so. The impulse in practically every other instance was to ignore the well-being of the community they had left behind because more typically, their exit from the 'hood was viewed as an escape.

Because teaching is a science, the educational system is particularly structured so that the ritual of learning can be controlled, and the outcome is predictable. For the longer part, education hinges on the live, intimate contact between teacher and student, but what merits attention is that the teacher is also transmitting nonverbal cultural cues. Such elements are passed on via the teacher's mannerisms, speech, dress, and attitude. Moreover, when the teacher speaks reverently of those perhaps, who have inspired him, or whom has made significant contributions to his profession or field of academia, it is usually dead, white, European males whose images are frozen into the student's mind.

In a very real sense, the images of these dead, white, European males are unconscious metaphors that serve to symbolize the greatness of white culture with the underlying assumption that no other culture is either valuable or worthwhile. That is precisely the reason why the vocabulary of academe is shaped around the experiences of the dominate culture. In this way, in addition to mastering an academic discipline, you also learn to celebrate the culture from which the knowledge sprung, and to idolize the men who evolved the culture.

In the world of academe, the greatest celebration is graduation, but for the brothas who graduated from college during the 70s, it also represented an abrupt break from their own culture. As college-educated, they were now the reborn highborn of the corporate manor, and as such could never go home again because a new social hierarchy of white picket fences beckoned. Cut loose from his own customs and values, the 'made' brotha' became, for all practical purposes, a corporate mystic------a highly paid wanderer who was conflicted emotionally. They, ultimately, recognize that no matter how great a particular field of study is, if it fails to influence you on a personal level, then it is more of a catastrophe than a reward. All education should serve as a function of your own culture so that it better instructs you how to preserve your own values, and how to perpetuate your sense of community. Otherwise, you became a mutant.

These newly-minted negroes, by no means, lack an understanding of the needs of the 'hood, but since that they are not free of the misconceptions about their own people, they find much more interest in white, genteel society where they become patrons of the arts, donating money to the local theatre. Investing in a museum or the opera is less forbidding to them than investing in the clean-up of the 'hood.

Dig this. The point here is not to disparage either education or upward mobility. Instead the 'diss' is against the 'inner voice' that grows out of education and upward mobility because while education may provide the text for your life, and while upward mobility may offer the subtext for your life, it is the inner voice that will decide the context for your life.

While both education and upward mobility consists almost exclusively of info and direction received outside of your mind's eye, your true feelings and compassion grow out of your inner voice. If the whole world is a stage, then your inner voice is the psychological prop needed to keep you in character, and specific to this notion is that if your inner voice is a parody of your own culture which represents who you truly are, then you will treat all your primary, traditional customs as comic.

It bears noting that learning is more influenced by one's cultural experience than it is by any choice of school, and the argument can be made that an education that subverts the culture of the learner reduces him because the orthodox fashion of imparting knowledge to students has always been to teach them that the knowledge will complete them, that it will expand the boundaries opened up for them by those who had their best interests in mind, and that it must be learned for the primary good of all.

Ironically, though, no matter their views on the African-American community at-large, the educated brothas adopt two main suppositions: (1)) that they are better than those left behind, and (2) that they have no responsibility for what goes on in the 'hood. One is based on arrogance; the other, ignorance. Either way, it upsets the traditional concept of carrying your community with you regardless of where you go.

A distinction must be made here in the cause-and-effect of education as taught in the context of race. Routinely, blacks have always viewed education as a tool that would permit them to engage themselves more fully in improving the conditions under which they live whereas white people tend to see education as a weapon which grants them the nearly unlimited potential to stand back and to make judgments. As a consequence, the sheepskin is merely an embellishment, the crowning ornament in their ability to impose their will upon the world.

Meanwhile as the educated brothas of the 70s lost their vision and failed to keep step with what was going on in their communities, their image became more tragic than heroic. Even their appearance turned shocking as these new, black, corporate types made an even more physically eloquent statement of defection by shaving off their mustaches. What cultural treachery!

It's not that we black men take excessive pride in our mustaches, but it is a mark of distinction that we preserve. If nothing else, it implies that we are not gay, and in the hood what other reason do you need? It is almost a shock to see a straight brotha without that patch of facial hair over his lip, and it would take terrible shaving accident to make him cut it completely off, but these corporate brothas did. A clean face was almost the badge of admission to the corporate world, and it was a powerful part of the old boy network, but it was not synonymous with any segment of the brotha-man culture, except among the sissies who played the clean face role to the maximum.

So now, there was a new image: the clean-shaved, suit and tie brotha, the image most digestible to white America. This was our cult of heroes, black tokens, window—dressers of renown. Whereas only a select few of the establishment men would achieve any success on a par with their white counterparts, virtually all of them were at odds with the values of who they were and the communities they had deserted.

While black folks can usually place the sundry misdeeds of white America within a particular era of our history such as (1) The Slave Era, (2) The Jim Crow Era, (3) The Civil Rights Era, and (4) The Black Power Era, we missed what was happening during The Corporate Negro Era. Like damsels-in-distress, we were so caught up in the esteemed behavior of the white hero as he vowed to use his money to help us out of our sticky situation that we never understood that these new niggas were the surrogate-heroes who were to take over the role black preachers had always held in the black community.

This manipulation. While it did involve the social metamorphosis of a select group of black males, it was unlike most conversions since the new brothas were physically separated from the group they were supposed to control. However, the inevitable gimmick was that the miraculous transformation of these surrogate-gatekeepers would be so awe-inspiring that everyone would aspire to it.

One idea that was hardly new was the destruction of self-love which was the intended consequence of a wholly Euro—centric education. These brothas, lacking the love of self, or the ability to sympathize with the plight of their people, would, at the price of making them more pompous, help to destabilize the ghetto.

These establishment brothas, domesticated by their own self-interests, and further as a matter of principle, trumpeted America's benevolence, elaborating in their persons just how great the country was. These brothas were, in effect, an extension of white America.

SOURTIME BOOKS

In the 1970s, the goal of making black America more productive was curtailed by cost, and given the wide range of other government expenditures, it became a much better idea to make them dependent, and to further this goal, welfare dollars began to rival the cost of public schooling.

What was hoped for was that dependence would begat submissiveness because hardly ever does one bite the hand that feeds it. At least that was what was hoped for, and given the ever-present hostilities between the government and black America, welfare was conceived of as a facilitating mechanism, and swept along by its own rhetoric that "one could trap more bees with honey than with shit", white America attempted to unite black America through benevolent paternalism. And these suit-and-tie brothas were to become the legitimate purveyors of "what Mr. Charlie can do for you if you are good". The Santa Claus Syndrome.

In this context, the government was Santa and these suit-and-tie brothas were his little, black elves. Occasionally, the suit-and-ties would appear to be autocratic, but mainly their task was to present a 'visual' for their bossman, a sort of real-life, eye-popping aesthetic experience that would ooh and ahh black adults in the same way that a Christmas display at the mall would mesmerize small children, and using an assortment of visual toys----their car, their women, their money---these elves produced a very pleasing picture.

In practice, though, the Santa Claus Syndrome was more than just a bright idea by the government, or a way for the elves to make a name for themselves because Uncle Sam knew precisely what he wanted and would accept nothing less. These 'look-at-me' brothas, evolved organically from a western-style education, were developed to adjust the psychological and emotional life of the ghetto by invigorating them with the fantasy of middle-class niggerdom. Uncle Sam wanted to manufacture a never-never land, a black fairytale existence where they could reside if they played by the rules. However, the ulterior motive was to forestall black folks' sense of impending doom by instilling them with false hope.

Okay, here is the deal. Santa's elves awarded the government the luxury of two very distinct and profound changes in the hood. One, it once more gained control of the black image, and secondly, it had just granted itself the ability to control the external urges of dark America. And that was only the start. Nonetheless what was most compelling about this 'double trouble' was that having a buffer, white America could now safely gauge the mood of the far-distant, ghetto blacks by measuring it against the mood of the nearby black middle-class. This was true because the stability of the black middle-class was related to how well they kept the black riff-raff out, so by comparing the tension between the two groups, white America could make calculations and predictions about whether or not to expand certain social experiments.

Suddenly, black America became more predictable which was just as well because as the middle-class sought to distance itself from the lower class, they became fearful of losing out to the new black working class-----the domestics, the garbagemen-----who struggled to get ahead. Increasingly, the working class was eyed with suspicion, but as the middle-class amassed more wealth, they felt the best way to preserve their coveted status would be to favor laws that kept other blacks in their places.

And that was exactly what Uncle Sam desired since now they had someone to do their dirty work for them.

Chapter Eight

THE WORLD IS A GHETTO

The myth that grew out of the black middle-class image was a paradox. Of a certainty, the black middle-class was white America's response to the Civil Rights Movement, but it was also a dress rehearsal for the agonizing dilemma that would result as this segment of black society tried to establish its own cultural objectives. The choice was racial identity or group security.

In the 70s, the black middle-class was still too young to have developed its own real nobility, so in their new, ultra-patriotism, they eagerly draped themselves in the antics of the national anthem, and black bourgeois magazines such as Jet and Ebony played to this elitist vision. As the middle-class became both the cream of colored society, and the new face of black America, black newspapers also played their part, opting to become theatrical rather than inquisitive, serving up page after page of middle-class brothas and sistea huddling over 6:00 cocktails, or proudly throwing debutante balls for their sweetheart daughters.

In hindsight, it would be premature to characterize the middle-class as black power-brokers since they were altogether controlled by white America. In virtually everything, they were the mouthpiece of their puppet-masters, and this was no more evident than in the NAACP, the most important black organization ever. Despite its image, The NAACP was founded by white people, mainly Jewish ones. In fact, at the founding of the organization only one member, W.E.B. Dubois, was black. A further fact is that the NAACP was the personal 'keepsake' of the Springarn family with brothers Albert and Joel serving successively as president from day one until 1971. Prior to 1971, no black had ever held a position of real authority in the NAACP with the exception of Walter White, who was secretary from 1931-1955.

At best the NAACP was a re-enactment of the earlier abolitionist movement during slavery, a part of the old tradition where whites ultimately decided the remedy when they had received no injury. As Fredrick Douglass once remarked, "the best one suited to speak was the one who had received the injury."

The NAACP was cut from the same cloth, but have you heard this one about the NAACP and their most famous case. Well, check it out. What is most striking about <u>Brown v Board of Education</u> is that we applaud its triumph as the result of the legal prowess of Thurgood Marshall. However, the true cause of the victory was a lot more complicated.

The conspiracy started with Felix Frankfurter, a Supreme Court Justice, who had been the director of the NAACP for 18 years, and due to a clear conflict of interest should not have been allowed to hear any case brought by the NAACP to the Supreme Court. Yet nothing was said although everyone knew what was at stake.

First off, Frankfurter was in close touch with Marshall and other NAACP lawyers even though such contact was illegal, yet despite this obvious collusion, it was still not enough to change the preliminary vote of 6-3 against Brown, so murder became plausible to insure victory. Even the death of a Supreme Court Chief Justice could be explained away in context of what was at stake. And just what was at stake? The soul of black America.

Nevertheless, when the Supreme Court shut down its 1952-53 session with no announcement on <u>Brown</u>, it was slated for the next term, but the 6-3 vote remained the anticipated outcome as everyone knew, for a fact, that Chief Justice Vinson was committed to issuing an opinion against <u>Brown </u>and the NAACP. As a matter of fact, the announcement against Brown had already been established by an external Supreme Court memorandum.

So it came down to this. On October 12th, 1953, Vinson would convene a short hearing and then rule against Brown, but on September 8th, Vinson died suddenly of a heart attack. Vinson, at 63, was in excellent health and had no known health problems, but most insiders were not surprised. It was simply another one of those 'strange government heart attacks' that routinely occur during major political decisions, so, in DC, no one was shocked. (Remember the strange death of Ron Brown)

What happened after this is that President Eisenhower appointed Earl Warren as the new Chief Justice, and seven months later, with no prior notice, Chief Justice Warren issued an unanimous ruling for the NAACP instead of the anticipated 6-3 ruling against Brown! What else was so amazing about the ruling was that there was no legal evidence supporting it, and nothing was ever made of the accusation that Vinson had been 'removed' because he stood in the way of a favorable ruling for the NAACP. Vinson's son, Fred Jr, also met with a sudden death when he worked at The Department of Justice, and had hoped to uncover info on his father's sudden demise.

To his credit, Supreme Court Justice Frankfurter was never reprimanded for his unethical behavior of working to engineer a victory in a case where he had clear interests, and though Capitol Hill concluded that Vinson had indeed been murdered, there was never any investigation. It was some years later that Frankfurter was identified as the top dog of a powerful communist cell in Washington, and that he was the leader of all the communists in the Roosevelt administration. And it was the communist element in this country, along with the Jews, who were the primary movers and shakers that controlled the black middle class.

By why was Brown so damned important? Because it was a sinister plot to snap the black middle class of the 50s back into line. They had gotten a wee bit too uppity for their communist and Jewish masters, and had not done exactly what was required of them. As the black elite, these brothas, mostly teachers and preachers, had used their considerable clout to their own advantage rather than to further the designs of their white backers, and this disturbed the plans that were in place.

Again, Brown was important because the Jews and the communists decided to destroy the black middle class who, at that time, had become more independent that necessary, so the plan was to usher in the downfall of the black middle class, and then to place the rest of the black population under the absolute control of the government. In the meantime, the same Jews and communists would breed a new middle class who would do as they were instructed.

Brown was a calculated risk because it was known what integration would do, and once the new black middle class was established, it led one black educator to moan: "An entire generation of black youth has been deliberately tossed onto the scrap heap by false leadership which has left the black community disorganized and without hope".

In a 1989 interview with the principal of Dunbar High School in DC, Charles Lufton, noted sadly that "I had more influence on my students in the segregated environment........They used us as role models......I lost some of my finest teachers. Partly as a result of integration, our children do not have a positive sense of self."

Still today, we applaud Brown, but at its best, it was the ultimate display of swaggering, paternal, white arrogance. The black middle class had to be chastised and made an example of so that the new middle class would not make the same mistake. But there was more. Around this same time, Frankfurter had masterminded the decision in Shelley v Kramer which ultimately turned DC over to blacks. Shortly after the decision, in accordance with the ruling, real estate developers began the practice of "block-busting", where in DC one black family was moved on every block, and as can be imagined, whites quickly sold their homes at rock-bottom prices. Fortunes were made overnight as DC went from being lily-white to all black.

Additionally, as whites fled to the suburbs of Virginia and Maryland, their fear led to billions of dollars in sales of locks, alarm system----and guns. And now with the integrationism of Brown, the fear would increase even more, and once again, huge profits would be made.

Breaking with their white backers was perceived as a radical act, and the middle class of the 50s has to be chastened for it, but it was integration and the culture it spawned that doomed the rest of us.

Chapter Nine

Hood Rats

As far as it goes, image is the most powerful behavioral mechanism in the 'hood. There is nothing ambiguous about it. A tough one is indispensable, and when it comes to understanding the human condition in the 'hood, nothing is more serious. After image, everything else is secondary.

In every sense, the deeds of hood rats emerges from their image which is, strictly speaking, a social commentary drawn out of the myth of their family legend because in ghetto culture, the nature of how you get a headstart on the block is usually derived from the known or reputed oral accounts of your big brothers, uncles, or father's reputations. A well-armed image is a cultural heirloom that can be passed along among family and close kin, but no matter how 'bigged' up the image is, you are expected, at some point, to stop riding on the rep of your ancestors and to forge your own image.

In many ghetto families, the only thing passed down are the name and the image, and what will matter most in the end, despite their scars, battles, marriages, and failures, will be how close the sons have remained to the true image of their fathers. This is the essential element of success in the 'hood, and though it may appear incomprehensible to outsiders, the quality of life in the 'hood can be assessed by how much suffering gets done to preserve, live up to, or to enhance your image.

Image, then, is the premier social device whereby hood rats are measured, conceptualized, and given meaning, but since the reflexive character of image lacks the social reverence of identity, it is easy for a brotha to transform his identity, but harder to relinquish his image. That is why some brothas who identify themelves as Muslims, Christians, etc. still portray the image of a thug. Identity is like a hall of mirrors. Image is.

Identity can distort, and oftentimes it is not always a true reflection of the person as individuals can wittingly or unwittingly misidentify themselves as so many brothas have found out when they have unsuccessfully attempted to identify themselves as bonafide members of white, corporate America.

In the hood, the role of image helps to diminish anxieties about place because everyone contributes to the peace by walking their own tightrope. A ho is always a ho. A stick-up boy is always a stick-up boy. A playa is always a playa. Therefore, everyone know how to occupy their space. The danger comes in when hood rats try to experiment.

Whether coincidentally or not, 'hood rats will indelibly associate with conditions on the block they recognize as socially validating to them, and once they claim their set of conditions, they will automatically begin to ascertain who is either stronger or weaker than they are. This is the proverbial, urbanized hunter-gatherer instinct.

In the 'hood, social conditioning begins immediately after birth. From an early age, 'hood rats are much more apt to be 'doers', who, once they learn to walk, spend quite a bit of their waking hours in active participation of one pursuit or another in direct contrast to non 'hood rats whose traditional formative years are engaged with greater verbal instructions and cues.

Baby 'hood rats are more externally expressive and alert due to the fact that they make contact with their environment sooner, and as an unforeseen bonus, they are less apt to become traumatized by the ever-changing (worsening) of society because they tend not to suspect their biological disadvantages as much as they do the shortcomings of the physical environment. (That's why when things go wrong, white people blame themselves. Black folks blame society.)

Quite naturally, in an environment where the universally agreed upon response is to 're-act', the technical ability 'to do' is as valued as computer literacy, and that, unarguably goes to demonstrate why bigger, faster, and stronger are the ultimate 'hood qualities.

Isolated and cut off from mainstream America, the 'hood established a subculture unique to the whole world, placing great emphasis on Eubonics as the required language, Motown as its cultural soul, and the church as its center.

At the same time, however, white America had just experienced the most prosperous 30 years in its entire history. 1945-1975 had turned out to be a golden era for the American mainstream, and there was plenty of spending money in the hands of white folks. With money to burn, Uncle Sam spent untold billions on the construction of new suburban malls and new highways to get to them. Unsurprisingly, not a red cent of this post-war wealth was distributed to the 'hood. In response, our Eubonics grew more pronounced, our music more personal, and our religion more private. (perhaps the greatest paradox of our lifetimes is this: 'how in the hell is it possible that a powerless people could be enveloped by such a powerfully negative image'?!)

Nonetheless the 'hood, unremittingly grim, was nothing more (or less) than the evolutionary ass-end of

The Great White Society with both the harsh environment, and even harsher white men as antagonists. In the 'hood, there was never any 'all things being equal' to be considered, and the government could identify no viable reason to regulate affirmative action for black America since it could never be determined exactly what pillar of mainstream society would be upheld by their uplift. "Hood rats proved, once and for all, that democracy was not equipped with the social or political muscle to compete with its own shortcomings.

In nearly every quarter of while America, nothing provoked Uncle Sam to acknowledge that class differences, second only to 'cracker chauvinism' would strap black America to a constitution with a closet full of rattling skeletons.

SOULTIME BOOKS

One of the most obvious displays of class differences is evident in the oddly cool manner by which young, black schoolchildren can confront the alphabets and fashion them into Eubonics, and though this cultural interpretation of the ABCs may confound scholars, it is no less than a major activity by which a people attempts to discover themselves in the nature of things. Eubonics, to the youth, or anyone else versed in it, is the exclusive license to dispense your voice in a way that makes perfect sense to you. Taking cultural possession of the alphabets is as visionary as the present-day bastardization of the King's English was vital to the American colonists' new definition of themselves.

There is little doubt that in this country, one of the most coveted rewards of the ABCss are paycheck stubs because there is even less debate about proper grammar being the concrete from which the foundation of your financial life will be poured. Still, at the core of language rests the only catharsis that may help unclog our history since words are cast with a keen focus on breathing your own culture, color, and meaning upon the language you speak. Hood rats don't merely speak with their mouths. We talk through our being. That's why we need our hands to converse. They demonstrate the passion and color or what we're intending to say when the bland ABCs are not expressive enough.

Accordingly, we were compelled to reinvent the "Do—Re-Me of the music scale so that our music would not be as bland as white bread. In everything we have inherited from Euro-American culture, we have had to untangle it, and then square off against those in white

America who either laughed at or cursed at the razzle-dazzle, urban spin we put on everything, but there is more to the story than meets the eye because in universal lore, nothing is ever lost. Maybe, black folks are simply restoring the magic to the ABCs since after all, it was brothas, the Sumerians, who invented the alphabets.

Chapter Ten

The Big Bang Theory

And though the news was not well received, 'hood rats had to deal with the notion that the reason they were culturally constrained in their communities was due to the Big Bang which is the theory that the neighborhoods in which they lived were once a part of the larger society, but had been separated from other geographical areas by the fiery explosion of white racism.

Knocked out of the universe of community, the 'hood was kicked around like the loose pebble it had become. Other communities in the universe revolved around the axis of big business and national government, but not so the 'hood. However, if you triangulate the position of the hood against the positions of the federal government and the banking institutions, it becomes apparent that the 'hood was meant to die. Cut off from the rest of the social universe, 'hood rats discovered that "Doing for Self" was a 'light bulb' moment in the 'hood, but lacking direction, many early attempts brought about our moral demise. And the need to understand this phenomenon is imperative.

It would seem curious today that commercial radio had a hand in sparking the current loose morality that our beautiful women so wantonly exhibit, but it is as much a fabric of radio's irresponsible behavior as anything else. And it had nothing to do with suggestive lyrics.

Radio was one of the first commercial venture that gave voice to the black community, and in its own way, during its heyday, radio was as ubiquitous as television would later become. Nonetheless, for a while, radio powered the 'hood, delivering music and news, and pushing wine, beer, cigarettes, and pork on the 'hood.

Without the authoritative voice of our doctors, we were never apprised of the risk pork and other high-salt foods would have on our health. With our educators on the other side of the tracks, there was no voice of protest against the killer foods that were pushed across the airwaves. Although it was initially seen as harmless advertising, it would one day serve as the greatest detriment to our collective health. If the hood had not been devoid of concerned doctors, we would have learned early of our genetic predisposition for hypertension, diabetes, and stroke, but we were never put on notice.

No one bothers nowadays to mention that it was during the golden age of black radio (the 70s) that cheap commercials help deliver sistas to their present spell of immorality. In other words, what contributed to the occasion of black women becoming strippers and

Hoochie-Mamas was the social irresponsibility of commercial radio.

Again, with our educators out of sight in their middle class homes with their white wives, there was no one else available to fight the dirty war for the maintenance of our moral standards, so as part of their job, local DJs, with their smooth talk and glib lines, constantly invited sistas out to night clubs to participate in Hot Legs, Big Butt, or wet T-shirt contests. There was no need apparently for sistas to understand the implications of their actions, but once the idea matured in their heads that they could cash in our their physical assets, displaying themselves in public soon became another way to get a dollar. Soon, sistas were not just showing their asses in club, they started shaking 'em on the strippers' pole.

And it wasn't just radio. All hype aside, building a name for itself was a huge task for the 'hood, and in order for the enormous production to work, 'hood rats needed an error-free agenda. What developed was anything but that. Cursed from the start with a negative image and a lack of leadership, smooth sailing could scarcely be expected. Anyway, what emerged was CPT. Colored People's Time!

Ultimately, what happened is that instead of making an attempt to become commercially viable to the mainstream, 'hood rats, using CPT as a socio/economic barometer condensed the activities of the white macrocosm down into a black microcosm, hoping to invent our own system of economics from these white sparks.

In contrast to playing the stock market, 'hood rats invented the art of playin' da numbers. The speculative aura and appeal were identical, and as equally alluring. Before long, CPT had saturated the 'hood, and 'hood rats were parlaying their attributes and skills into scaled down imitations of their proper use.

For example, you could take a 'hood rat who possessed the exact, same skills as Richard Petty, or any other race car driver, but in a world based on CPT, NASCAR would be unthinkable, so the brotha does the 'hood equivalent: *he becomes a getaway driver for a stick-up crew.* The skills are precisely the same, but the brotha defines himself differently in relationship to those skills, and what this so aptly demonstrates is the extent to which the individual values himself.

Another example. Imagine two males---one black, one white---who both possess the gift of gab. It is highly possible that in the macrocosm of the white world, the white kid will use his communication skills to maximum effect by becoming a motivational speaker. But what will the brotha do in the microcosm? What else? He will use his great gift of persuasion to turn some sista out, influencing her to become a prostitute. In CPT, the brotha sees no real advantage to using his skills to motivate a sista to go to college to become a lawyer or a doctor or a president, so he tricks her into becoming a ho.

To white America, CPT was simply a nigga aphorism that showed off the secret to how certain our ignorance was, and what that meant to white folks was that we were the perfect lab rats. What else was particularly true at the time was that the 'hood was the ideal maze, and as evolving colonizers, white folks now possessed a laboratory that would permit them to eliminate the mystery of how people would act under the thumb of a colonizing power.

As practicing imperialists, white America had a huge appetite for this sort of knowledge, and the 'hood was a fluid and dynamic environment where we unwittingly offered a scientific and psychological examination on what total displacement did to a people. We offered this country a most detailed and systematic evaluation of the effectiveness of colonization, and it exploited us with the same eagerness it would use on their overseas colonies.

With hardly any delays, brothas and sistas blossomed from slaves of the American empire to subjects of the American empire. The 'hood was indeed cordoned off, but there was no attempt to incorporate us into the democratic mainstream. We were annexed, and what came next was tainted drinking water, lead-based paint, and arsenic-infected soil, all of which resulted in the beginning of our debilitating health issues.

Frankly, half of what we believed about white folks was patently wrong, and the parts we did get right, we foolishly made a ceremony out of them, but the most disturbing mistakes of our collective history has been CPT, and the old-pie-in-the-sky.

After the Big Bang, the hood went on life support, and up until the time of our imminent demise, white liberals, doing tremendous second-guessing, continued to stick social catheters and political feeding tubes down our throats as a matter of conscience. They didn't want to lose their privilege of being portrayed as "the other white folks" as opposed to the mean neo-conservative right-wingers.

But when did America become really, really become afraid of us? Simply put, when, among other things, they determined that their inability to destroy us was not from a lack of trying.

BONEFIRE BOOKS

Throughout the history of peoples, there has been ample evidence that _observation_ can change behavior, but despite all the detriment that has befallen the hood, nothing has ultimately led to any significant modifications of hood attitude and behavior. In fact, there is nothing complex at all in recognizing how damaging our lifestyle choices have been, and since there has been nothing inconsequential regarding either the swiftness or the structure of the punishment, we should have, out of necessity, started behaving better a helluva long time ago. Yet no.

Pointing-our-fingers-at-someone-else has become the traditional pseudonym for anything that does not go right with us, and since we have never learned to be team players, the emotional detachment induced by CPT grants us the surreal habit of being able to witness detriment occur to our neighbor and not to understand the larger process at work. This is our fix, the proverbial monkey on our backs. We don't embrace the notion that if it can happen to him, it can happen to me. We are too individual for that.

Hood rats have never attempted to hide the fact that we have patiently observed our higher-than-expected mortality rates due to cigarettes, alcohol, unprotected sex, and other high-risk behavior, and though we clearly understand how we contribute to our misery by pursuit of such detrimental activities, we don't see them as especially risky since they occur because of private, individual choices. Unfortunately, this subconscious notion has tricked us into believing that our collective self-destruction is an individualized snapshot of us being picked off one by one.

In the hood, CPT has produced the troubling trend of hood rats having a general faith in not believing what we see, or the more potentially dangerous concept of believing that nothing *worse* will happen to us.

In the hood, self-destructive behavior is the social template by which we attack the chronic conditions of our hopelessness which means that we will continue to take chances rather than make cures.

50 years ago, CPT was a cultural paradigm that allowed us to define ourselves by giving us a new 'home-grown' way to look at ourselves. Essentially, CPT was a zoot-suited, wheeling-and-dealing, free-styling

acknowledgement of our march to a different drummer, but upon closer examination, it did not point out our need for a concrete image. After all, what need was there for an image since we had been conditioned not to believe what we saw anyway.

Chapter Eleven

THE BIG BOOM THEORY

With scarcely any exceptions, the white media has done little to temper their broadcast of our image as savages, and the black newspaper and magazines that have shown an interest in doing so have been wholly subdued in their efforts. The belief that they could somehow reshape our negative image before it got any worse has confounded them because for white America, and its infatuation with greed will never allow normal depiction of us as long as fear sells. Sex sells, but not as good as fear, and our negative image fuels the sales of security paraphernalia.

For a great many corporations, the negative image of black America has become a sure-fire formula for success. This visible, negative image of the black man has been enough to jumpstart the economy and in the process, to encourage a whole cottage industry of its own. Guns have always sold better than butter, and no doubt the media would band together to ride the coattails of this 'check-in-the-mail' phenomenon, and as soon as they did, the political push for stricter laws emerged. As a direct extension of this mindset, money would flow into the coffers of private construction companies to build more prisons.

It may have been illegal to sell the black man outright, but no one could denounce white America for selling his image. And this was good. To the media big-wigs in the North, control of the black image represented a chance (finally) for them to squeeze profits out of the former slaves as the South had already been privileged to do.

It goes without saying that the media had no fierce loyalty to the laws designed to protect the black man. To them, it was childish romanticism because they understood that a great headline tended to supercede the law.

When the Big Boom started in earnest, it was decided that for once, Hollywood lacked the intensity to either form---or to deform---the bold feat needed to make the new image of the black man to appear biological or genetic in origin. True, Hollywood had made the most of its opportunities to bash the image of the black man in America, and it had to be roundly congratulated for both the spectacular job it had done in Gone With The Wind when the image of a head-scratching, happy-go-lucky, foot-shuffling buffoon was needed, as well as for the shit it had done with the Blaxploitation movies. But, for once, Hollywood lacked the heart for what was to come next. This was Armageddon. Or at least, the early phases of it.

Most of the time, the white media, on the whole, encountered little difficulty in exploiting the image of black America which was not surprising given the immense power and influence of journalists, writers, and other media-related personnel, the vast majority of whom were more than happy to take full advantage of the astonishing 'make-work' attitude of their employers.

By all measures, the media should have been ecstatic. And why not? Here was an assignment they couldn't screw up. When the nigga-bashing started, the ghetto was in worse condition than ever before, and with practically no exceptions, the hood rats were victimized brutally. Had the impulse been to provide relief for the hood, it would have been during the 'Second Reconstruction', the period during Roosevelt's New Deal era under the auspices of the Civil Works Administration. The CWA was founded by Executive Order where the President transferred 400 million dollars into a government program to provide jobs for individuals out of work due to the depression. People all over the country applied to join the CWA, and the program was so successful that another 950 million dollars was allocated for it.

In theory, the CWA was simply a measure to instill pride in people who refused government assistance, and though there were examples of men sweeping streets that didn't need to be swept, half a million miles of highways were constructed. Thousands of bridges were built; school, churches, and hospitals sprung up and almost 600 airports were built, not to mention the many municipal parks and other recreational facilities that emerged all across the nation. The entire face of America was given a facelift by the CWA. America was truly a pretty bitch now.

Additionally, they were jobs set aside for teachers, and 10% of CWA's budget was earmarked for white-collar workers. Even artist were supported via The Public Works of Art Program, and historians were paid to go on digs with archeologists. Thanks, in part, to Eleanor Roosevelt, there were programs for women who drew salaries for sewing and other home economic projects.

Guess what? The hood didn't get shit! And in typical fashion when black folks in Jackson, Mississsippi petitioned for CWA money to put brothas to work fixing up the 'hood, the Mayor said that he "would not give them a damned thing." And so it was all over America. Everyone benefitted from the CWA-----except black people.

In total, the CWA, during 1933, with its 1 billion dollar expenditures could have spruced up the 'hood, and helped to eliminate the blight and desperation, but since white America decided that black America had no pride, there was no need to include them in the good works of the CWA. Instead, it was determined that welfare was a better experiment for us.

White America wanted our dependency.

In most respects, this was the ultimate disrespect. White America forced us to watch them feast and wouldn't even throw us a bone, but that was not the first or last time. Some thirty years later after John F. Kennedy was ushered into The White House, money was set aside by the government to revitalize the inner cities. Schools and hospitals were to be built, roads were to be paved. Finally, the hood was going to be cute, and there would, at last, be a chicken in every pot.

Not so fast. What happened was The Space Race. Russia was just about ready to put a man in outer space before America did. America had somehow fallen behind in this international contest of "get-to-moon-before-you-do", and the whole world was watching. World domination was at stake as the winner of this high-stake competition would have the clout to influence the other nations to choose either Democracy or Communism as their socio/political agenda. To Uncle Sam, beating the Russian to outer space was merely another brick in the wall to halt the growing red menace of communism.

This edict to beat Russia to the moon became etched in stone, and any and all available money, including the money set aside for the hood, was diverted to NASA and the space race. America's pride was at stake and saving face was much more important to them than saving us. What more was to be expected. Hell, this was a country with a congress that had failed to pass an anti-lynching bill, so how could we expect them to help us when we couldn't get them to stop killing us.

Chapter Twelve

AMERICA, LOOK WHAT YOU'VE
DONE

What we have here is the abject failure of those who make the laws to keep in mind the laws of karma. Thanks to hard-hitting, soul-taking punitive laws, we are now experiencing the natural outgrowth of the seeds spawned by these draconian measures.

Ever heard the old adage about "the same thing that makes you laugh, makes you cry. Right now, we are at the crying part. No so very long ago, politicians and other law-and-order folks, were patting each other on the backs, and celebrating just how successful they had been at enacting the most stringent criminal laws in history. Now, we shed tears because we are currently living through the holocaust conjured up by these laws.

I cannot even begin to imagine how many times some judge in some courtroom, somewhere in America has looked down on someone he was about to sentence, telling the guy about how 'actions carry consequences'. Well, what I'd like to say right now to those judges is "that's back at ya! If I was a drinking man, I would raise a glass in toast and say, "Here's looking at you, kid, your fucking chickens are coming home to roost!"

There was a bank robbery yesterday in a town a few miles from Charlotte where the robber decided to shoot it out. In the process, he was killed. He held court in the streets. Get used to it, because this is a trending lifestyle in the criminal world. A'int nobody got time to go to prison no mo', so crooks are taking it upon themselves to see to it that they get a fair trial in the streets. Blood is going to flow because what possible judicial incentive can there even remotely be when you know before you even plan the crime that there is no parole? Given that reality, getting killed in a shootout offers a double bonus. One, you get to avoid prison time, and secondly, you get the chance to take others, preferably the police, to hell with you.

This threat is very real, and it is one that has been in the incubator, warming up since the seventies. I remember Comrade George Jackson, who was killed while in prison, saying in his book of that era about how he was going to shoot it out with the cops if they ever tried to arrest him again. He said that he was going to put us such a firefight that the cops who finally did manage to slay him would get congressional medals of honor for outstanding valor!

And now for a moment of confession. I know many who are of the same mind. I no longer break the law. Thank God, because if I still did, this is what I would do. I'm tired of running from the police and if I had committed a crime, and they were looking for me. I would not run a single step. I would strap up, meaning I would get a vest of explosives, and walk right into the police department, and blow the bitch up. I realize how harsh and unforgiving that may seem, but that it precisely what I would do. No ifs, ands, or buts about it. I would feel like so many others do, that I don't have a choice but to hold court in the streets.

Even in diplomatic circles, when two countries are embroiled in a conflict, the country on the losing end must be allowed a way to save face. He will concede, but he must be permitted to save face. Well, back in the days, parole, probation, and leniency, were all "plums" that permitted a criminal to concede and still have something to look forward to in court. But not now.......so why even bother when you can hold court in the streets where you can be the judge, the jury, and executioner.

If you wonder why the streets are so unsafe, don't take the easy way out by merely pointing at the actions of the powerless without assessing the damage caused by those in power whose took away the safety valves, and opened the floodgates.

The police, no matter how well-founded their intentions, will be helpless to stop crime because they don't understand the psychological culture of what is happening right under their noses, let alone the emotional mindset that engineers everything.

Anyway, just like in the Bob Marley song, "every day the bucket goes down to the well, one day the bottom will fall out." Well, in this society, the bottom has fallen out. So how much worse is it gonna get? Who knows? You know it's pretty darn bad any time you live in a so-called civilized society, the greatest on earth, and you are terrified of going to court. At one time, this proverbial 'day in court' was one of the most famous linchpins of modern-day America. Now, it is the most feared and unpopular.

What else must be noted is this and it is vital. Prisons are bad, okay, and no one wants to go back but no one wants to be poor in the free world either. In a nutshell, you have hell fixing to break loose because when you have terrible laws on one hand, and lawless prisons on the other, what you have then is a vow that some prisoners make upon their departure from prison. This "out the door" don't-take-me-alive, vow becomes the bread and butter of his life. But what anyone outside the culture will probably never understand is that this vow not to be taken alive by the police provides something that is both prized and priceless: Absolute Freedom!

Believe it or not, but this "Don't Take Me Alive" Philosophy allows a man to do whatever the fuck he pleases. He knows what's in it for him, and once he works out the kinks of his willingness to die, then what is there to stop him for doing as he chooses? He has no restraints. He fears nothing. He is totally free.

America, your chicken are coming home to roost.

For anyone who mistakenly believes that things have gotten better in the criminal justice system, then here's something you need to know. It hasn't. And guess what" You had better brace yourselves for what it to come next. It's not going to be pretty. Most jail-breaks aren't.

At some point, perhaps, in the very near future, what is going to occur is that ex-convicts are going to start busting their friends out! Do you find this unthinkable? If so, you had better rethink the concept. Whether you know it or not, but the strongest bond between men is forged in prison, and these friendships cemented in the blood, sweat, and tears of an agonizing, organized hell, endure. These bonds, sometimes, are more stronger than family, and more vital than religion.

Sometimes, it's not merely enough to send your comrade a few dollars, a few pictures of naked women, a card at the holidays. Sometimes, you want him out! I personally know convicts, who, once released from prison, robbed a bank and used the proceeds to hire a lawyer in an effort to get their friend out. And, by no stretch of the imagination was this an isolated case. However, that was back in the days when a man could still get a fair shake in court. In today's political climate, such an effort would be like throwing good money away, so why not just bust him out.

Let me relate a personal account that shows that people are not afraid of busting friends out of prison. In 1985, after I had been sentenced to prison for a crime I didn't commit, I was in the mountains at a little, small, gun camp. Anyway, there was this white guy that was there, and he had been fascinated that I had been a bank robber. He loved to listen to my "war stories" about robbing banks. I even sent home for my transcripts of my bank robberies trials. He cherished them. And then one day just before he was to be released, he told me that he would break me out if I let him rob banks with me. He saw me as some bank-robbing hero, and he was dead serious about busting me out. Plus, he already had it all planned out—and guess what, it would have worked!

I turned him down because I thought Oprah was coming to my rescue. I had written Oprah, 60 Minutes, Geraldo, The NAACP, The ACLU, etc. about my case. *I was innocent!* I didn't deserve to be in prison. I really, truly believed that once my story was heard...........Anyway, no one came for my black ass, and I ended up serving over a decade in prison for a crime I did not know a damned thing about. Should've taken my white friend up on his offer, but I found out that he didn't need me after all. He became a pretty good bank robber on his own. I forget where I was locked up at, but I was reading the newspaper and, VOILA, there was a big article about him. He was real smooth. I felt proud. I was sad that he had gotten busted, but I was prouder than a motherfucka that he was true to the game.

I guessed I said all that to say that it doesn't take much to want to knock a prison over. I will give another testimony. I recall a point during one of my earlier bids where a whole lot of convicts admired the Palestinians who used to hijack planes and then exchange the hostages for their comrades in captivity. I mean this was really given a lot of thought, and several guys I knew had a list of the convicts' names they would ask for in an exchange.

Here is another tidbit to ponder, if you dig the truth. There was this Jewish gangsta that I had bidded (served time) with in the fed joint in Atlanta. We were not extremely close, but we were aware of each other, mainly because of my gig in the kitchen. Anyway, just under a decade later, we met again. This time in the local jail. This was in 85, and I had been back in state prison for two years for the crime I did not commit, and I had won a hearing due to an appeal I had filed. Anyway, my old, Jewish acquaintance had just gotten busted for smuggling in a few tons of reefer, and was in the jail cell when I got there.

He was old, and when he used to get high, (He had weed in the cell), he always talked of dying in prison, something that haunted him immensely. Shit, I was in virtually the same boat, but knew that with the right lawyer, I could beat this rap, so I offered him a proposition. He knew about my case, and I promised him that if he would hire me a good lawyer that could whip this case for me, that I would break him out of prison! I meant it and I honored it with my "convict" word.

As fate would have it, I was called to court before C. could get the lawyer for me, and my worst fears were confirmed. I lost at the hearing. If, by chance, I would have gotten the attorney, and would have beaten the charge, I would have honored my word, and I would not have given a damn about where he was, I was coming to get him.

Marion, until recently, was the toughest federal prison, and when I was there, there was a respect for a convict who had been there. There had even been a big article on him in The Rolling Stone, called The Gangster of Love. This guy had two women, (a mother, and a daughter,) to attempt to bust him out of prison. And if that wasn't enough, he ran for President of The US from his prison cell! At any rate, when the mother failed in her attempt, getting shot and killed in the process, the daughter took it upon herself to continue the quest.

In prison, the thing most constant on a prisoner's mind is freedom. *Remember that.* I remember a guy that stayed in the same cellblock where I lived, and one night when it was time for Soul Train, I ran excitedly to his cell, giving him the good news. Soul Train was now airing. He looked me in the eyes and said that the last thing he wanted to see was sexy women. He said that he had a life sentence which meant that his career with women was officially over. That, in and of itself, was almost enough to make you want to escape. The next time I saw Biggs was about five years later at another prison. He was on the Mental Health Unit, the so-called 'nut ward'. He was a zombie, so heavily medicated that he didn't even know who I was. Looking at him, I thought that it would have much better for him to had tried to escape than to have let this happen to him. He was, for all practical purposes, dead. As a friend, I would have much rather to have seen him physically dead from an apparent escape attempt that to view him mentally and spiritually dead.

That was always the thing with brothas. We would rarely try to escape. We thought we were tough, so we would grit our teeth, and suffer. White convicts would jump the fence. Me, I didn't think twice about trying to get missing if I had half a chance to pull it off.

Damn! If we could have pulled off that escape from Petersburg in 76', that would have been one for the books. And we almost did it, and would have accomplished the mission, had it not been for someone telling on us. Snitching was almost unheard of back in the 70s, and virtually nonexistent in the prison system, but yeah, someone got us.

Man, I still get goosebumps from just reliving those moments. Like I said in another piece about the escape, I was scared although not scared in a cowardly fashion. No, this was the fear that men felt when they understood that death was right around the corner. Now, thanks to the new 'get tough' laws, convicts face another fear, one even greater than the fear I experienced at four in the morning, lying in damp gravel atop a two story prison building, desperately waiting for the flashing lights of our getaway car, informing us that it was a go. Can you imagine the fear that ensued when we realized that our getaway car was not coming? We were trapped outside the dorm, and could not get back in so there was nothing to do but continue the escape with the bad news that there would be no transportation and guns on the other side of the fence. We were, basically, abandoned, left to suffer whatever would come next.

What came next was the fear of getting shot with automatic weapons. So what could possibly be worse than a four a.m. execution? Well, it is the very real fear the convicts face of never, ever seeing their loved ones ever again! It is that one gnawing fear that will give way to 'the new hell' that awaits this country. And couple this with another very, very real fear that every convict lives with.

Right this moment, convicts fear Donald Trump. Know why? The public may not be aware of this but convicts certainly are. There is a law that certifies the wholesale death of convicts in the event this country is ever invaded by a foreign enemy. In that eventuality, the prisoners would be locked in their cells and gas will be administered through the air vents. What a lovely way to die. This is no old wives' tales, or a lost book from Mother Goose's fairy tales. It is a thing that convicts believe with all their hearts.

What would be a greater strategy than for an invading army to free the prisoners, many of whom would gladly take up arms against the country who had spit in their faces, and locked them away, throwing away the key. But even if the convicts didn't take up arms, it would be a logistics nightmare for America to attempt to round the prisoners up, and to fight a war at the same time. It was be anarchy!

With Trump in office, convicts are sweating, never sure if he will do something foolish, calling forth war. Things are already tense in the world of foreign affairs, and with the US and North Korea selling wolf tickets, who knows what the fuck might happen, and convicts might just decide not to stick around to find out. Busting out of jail is lot better than getting gassed while you are asleep in your cell.

Join the campaign to reform prison now. Your life depends on it.

For more of my work, go to www.soulfirebooks.com

For most of my life, I was the guy most wannabe thugs wished they could be. Officially declared a menace to society, I was sentenced to 30 years in federal prison for my role as mastermind of a series of daring bank robberies in the 70s. Two involved shootouts. One with the police. The other with a citizen in a bank parking lot where I narrowly missed being killed. While confined, I took part in an even more daring prison escape. Despite this seeming penchant for violence, I consoled myself with the notion that I was merely a poet trapped in a gangsta's body and oddly enough, this wasn't far from the truth as I had evolved from a family of teachers, four of whom taught English. As such, I learned, early on, to respect and to appreciate language since my grandmother was very strict and would not tolerate improper grammar under her roof.

From the start, there appeared to be a household conspiracy to convert me into a writer. By the time I was ten, I possessed a private library fit for a scholar, had a new typewriter, a big desk, and plenty of blank paper. By 11, I had mastered the dictionary, was a whiz at Scrabble, and was an honor roll student in school. At twelve, I had completed my first novel. By my 13th birthday, I had discovered hustling and I immediately dropped out of school and adopted the streets as my home. By 14, I was in reform school for assaulting a police officer. While there, I was a star journalist, the first black deemed smart enough to work in the print shop. I served one year and a day. Upon my release, with hardly any delays, I embarked on a personal crime spree, and at the age of 15, I was sent to prison where I was the youngest convict there. While in the Youth Center, I acquired my high school diploma at 16, wrote my first play, turned militant, and when released at 19, went to New York to join the Black Panthers. In New York, I discovered heroin. Writing and the revolution would both have to wait as a drug habit left little room for anything else. When I tired of being a junkie, I kicked my fascination with getting high, but years later would emerge as the alleged kingpin of a notorious heroin distribution ring. Finally brought down by the FBI and DEA in 1997, I again was sent to federal prison. This time I would be gone for a decade, but once more I turned back to what I had turned my back on: writing.

I studied journalism, started a writer's colony, mentored other aspiring prison writers. I edited and founded various newsletters, performed freelance editorial services for outside writers while quietly perfecting my craft. Hailed by some as one of the greatest prison writers ever, I was interviewed by numerous TV and print outlets. My writings have even been studied in an English class at a university where I was invited to lecture. While in the Atlanta Federal Penitentiary, I published two novels, but soured on traditional publishing after a deal gone bad with an independent publisher. I also developed two programs. One, PROJECT UPLIFT, which deals with drug-dealer addiction. The second, GIRLSMART, a community service program concerned with at-risk, teenaged, black girls. This program is a counter to the video vixen syndrome where sistas opt to employ their booties rather than their brains. Lastly, I have finally gone from wrong to "write!

www.soulfirebooks.com

www.ingramcontent.com/pod-product-compliance
Lightning Source LLC
Chambersburg PA
CBHW050353280326
41933CB00010BA/1448